365 DAYS TO AUTHENTICITY

365 DAYS TO AUTHENTICITY

Constance Holdip

authorHOUSE®

AuthorHouse™
1663 Liberty Drive
Bloomington, IN 47403
www.authorhouse.com
Phone: 1 (800) 839-8640

Published by AuthorHouse 07/30/2015

ISBN: 978-1-5049-0969-3 (sc)
ISBN: 978-1-5049-0968-6 (e)

Contents

This book is dedicated to my Lord and Savior Jesus Christ, my late loving parents, my sons, grandchildren, daughter-in-laws, sister-in-law and siblings. To the man that I have loved all of my life, I am grateful for what we share. A special thanks to my daughter who labored in editing my work. I also thank my friend, Karen, for her work in the final editing. I am grateful for the love and support of friends and mentors who have supported and blessed me. To every challenge, every triumph, every heart break, every person, every love, that has formed me, I am grateful for the journey!

Thank You!

Intro: 365 days to Authenticity

365 Days to Authenticity is an extension of my life coaching business Finding Your Authentic Path. I've worked in the helping profession for over 20 years.

In my early years I experimented a lot. I thought I wanted to be a nurse so I pursued nursing school. After a few years of working as a nursing assistant I wanted to tap into my artistic side. So I started a path in retail by going to a design school to become a buyer. That was a fun time in my life. I learned about art, interior design, fashion buying, and fashion writing. Additionally I learned floral design. After several years in that world, I searched for more meaning in my life. During that time my marriage ended in divorce. So I needed to take care of myself and my two sons. I went back to school and pursued a career in teaching. I worked as a substitute teacher for a year while seeking my degree. Soon I discovered that I wanted to teach people more than curriculum. The student's issues and how they responded to their problems was much more interesting to me.

I changed my major to social work. The years I spent working as a social worker turned out to be the most profound and rewarding work of my life. I worked with the homeless population earlier in my profession. In the last years in my career I worked with children with emotional and behavioral trauma. In addition while working with abused and neglected children my perspective about life changed. My gratitude expanded. I fully embraced life as a precious gift. I learned so much during those years about basic human needs. The year I spent working with hospice patients increased my knowledge in prioritizing. I learned that one of the most important things in life is to spend time with the people you love. I was able to witness people's last days on the earth while working in Hospice. They all wanted to spend those last days with their love ones.

In January of 2012 my mother became very ill. Our family decided that we would take care of our mother at home. She passed away three months later. It was truly one of my best gifts in life, being able to assist my siblings in taking care of her. It was a precious time for our family.

Before my mother's passing the Holy Spirit started to prepare me for transitioning out of social work into life coaching. I began learning about coaching while still working as a social worker. By the time my mother passed I had already created my coaching business Finding Your Authentic

Path. The time had come to transition out of social work and into life coaching. The timing was perfect. I could not have played a significant part in my mother's care without establishing a new beginning for myself.

I was inspired by my own transition to name my brand of coaching transitional coaching, assisting others through significant life events.

To many, it may appear that I've sailed out of one profession into another. But this is my journey and I believe that we all are endowed with multiple gifts. These gifts are to be used to glorify God.

The spirit of God led me to many avenues to pursue my passions. There are seasons in the natural world, but also seasons in a person's life. Seasons always represent change. By acknowledging and moving into those seasons I was led into my life's work.

I am not suggesting that everyone has to change their profession multiple times. We are all individuals and have different callings on our life. But listening for the call and acting upon it led me to some exciting adventures.

One of the major reasons why *365 Days to Authenticity* was written because I was constantly meeting people both in my professional and personal life who were not satisfied with their lives.

My biggest question was why? Why were so many people not really living the life they truly wanted to live?

I found many answers, but the greatest one was fear. Basically people felt like the life they were dreaming about was just a dream, not a reality. This saddened me I wanted to do something about it.

I also met people who were just exhausted, and felt tired most of the time. My thought was if people are tired all the time, when is it possible to have time to dream or even realize a dream?

The overwhelming thought in my mind was that many people were not really living authentically. I knew I wanted to address these issues in my business and this book. Making a New Year's resolution did not appear to be a recipe for success either. I wanted to share with others some life lessons that I learned over time that made a difference in my life.

I believe that living authentically is living a life that is true to you. Your original intent is the reason God created you.

In my coaching business, when a client is going through a life crisis I assist the client to not just survive through the change. But while they are going through the transition I teach them to use the crisis as an opportunity to get back to their authentic self.

That's what *365 Days to Authenticity* is all about taking a year's journey to refresh and challenge your old way of being. After examining your life, you can then make the adjustment by moving forward to a life that is authentic.

I invite you not to start the New Year with making empty resolutions, but to take the journey to finding real solutions that will affect the rest of your life.

I'm a Christian who believes that all life begins with our creator, and that receiving Jesus Christ as your Lord and Savior is the gift of life. Through this relationship I have been able to realize my authentic self.

It is my intention to serve others with all of the gifts that have been generously bestowed upon me. I hope this book will be a blessing to you as you travel to find your authentic path.

Everything begins with God! (Colossians 1:16 -17) Before you were brought into existence, you were a thought in the mind of God! He created you for His purpose. He endowed you with marvelous gifts that were designed specifically for your purpose in life. Your physical appearance, your size, shape, gender, height, and nationality are all a part of his divine design. Your personality, brain capacity, intelligence, creativity, interest, passions, and talents are all a part of your genius. You were created to bring a message to earth!

In the nano seconds it took for God to complete his thought of you. You were birthed into humanity! The family you were birthed into is your earthly vessel. A great celebration took place in the heavenly realm. There is promise in new life. A spirit wrapped into flesh has come to bring great gifts and talents to the world. That spirit is you!

We've all witnessed and benefited from great messengers. But in everyday life we share the good fortune of being touched by unsung heroes. They are the ones who are not famous but still profoundly affect our lives. These great people would be our mothers, fathers, pastors, friends, mentors, and teachers and siblings. These infectious spirits help build and support us throughout life.

Through love and support from the people who have been divinely placed into our lives we are able to understand the reason why we are here. No one accomplishes anything alone.

Some people show promise at a very early age. From the beginning they follow their path and manifest their purpose.

Then there are some individuals that go through personal struggles, however they manage to stay focus and blossom into their purpose. Yet still, there are others whose lives are full of jagged edges and profound adversity! Their stories are laced with incredible adversity from an early age. The hardship and pain that they endure is extremely difficult. These are the people when they become victorious and their stories are told inspire us to live without any excuses!

The journey to manifest purpose is paved with necessary challenges and obstacles. Pathways are as individual as snowflakes. All of their patterns are intricately and distinctively different from each other.

Decisions lead to pathways. Thoughts turn into actions, and actions transform the purpose into reality.

However in the day-to-day grind of life, what happens when we disconnect from our spirit? A lot of us travel far from the original intent, plan, and purpose we were born to fulfill! This happens all the time. We can get side tracked by daily life challenges.

When we drift away from our original purpose, life can become mundane, methodical, and in some cases a sense of hopelessness can set in.

365 Days to Authenticity is a guide to the journey back to your real self. Living authentically is not as mysterious as it seems, especially when practical application can be applied to everyday living.

Something terrible has happened to the present manner in which we live in modern times. Life has become complicated. It has become a gigantic matrix of commitments we must get done at any cost! The price we pay to get it done has disconnected people from the source of life. Many people believe that the accumulation of money and things in the material world is the end all be all.

Relationships have become a means to further business and to promote self. Life has become a shallow abyss for many who don't equate success with loving relationships, time to enjoy life, and time to serve others.

It is crucial in these times of high-speed technological advances and rapid changes in our world, to return to a simple and natural way of being. It is crucial to recover by investigating the original intent for being, and to put it into every day practice.

365 Days To Authenticity challenges readers to look deep from within and find a way back to their heart. 365 days offers you an opportunity to take a look at yourself with an open heart and open mind. It challenges you to focus on what changes and adjustments that you could possibly take to live a graceful and purely authentic life.

I think we have all experienced and can relate to feelings of being stuck or overwhelmed by life challenges.

Sometimes we stay in the familiar, even if it is painful, because it's safe. Living safe might get most of us through the hour, day, month, or year. But what happens to the quality of life when the familiar becomes an obstacle to living free?

Many of us go about our day with hefty schedules. After the New Year we add even more pressure to our lives by declaring empty resolutions. These resolutions have the appearance of forward moving, however after a few months the new resolutions fade away.

I don't think that what I am suggesting is new. Most of us realize and can identify with this crazy cycle. Then another year passes with the same familiar frustrations. Maybe just maybe you are at a place in your life that you are ready to do things differently. Could it be that this is your divine time to seize the moment? Carpe diem! Just by purchasing this book you have made a declaration. You are proclaiming that this is the year of no more empty promises. You are proclaiming this year as being the start of a new and dynamic beginning! Let this guide be your conduit for change. By making this declaration you are ready to do some real work that will advance your life to a powerful way of living. So roll up your sleeves, take a deep breath, and get ready to live honestly and authentically. Welcome to your new reality!

MONTH 1

January: Season of New Beginnings

Every year millions of people celebrate the New Year! People around the world celebrate the promise of new beginnings.

People participate in some kind of ritual. These rituals can range from a quiet evening at home, to people creating small gatherings, to huge and elaborate parties where the champagne flows like a river.

Some people choose to spend time in a spiritual atmosphere where they are honoring God with friends and family.

Then there are great cities such as Las Vegas, New York, and Paris that attract people who enjoy bringing in the New Year in a crowd and all of the noise of celebration that comes with it.

There is much anticipation with the coming of something new. I compare it to when a baby is born into a family everyone is waiting for the joy to enter into the world. Just like new life, the New Year feels like the promise of great things to come.

Expectations are high during this time, and people begin to make new plans for the future.

People begin to declare their new reality by stating what the New Year will look like for them. We call these declarations resolutions.

Webster's Dictionary describes New Year's resolution as a fixed determination; firm set on a course of action.

A key element to a New Year's resolution that sets it apart from other commitments is that it is made in anticipation of the New Year and new beginnings.

People committing themselves to a New Year's resolution generally plan to do so for the whole year.

It is interesting what Webster' Dictionary declares a resolution as a fixed determination, to take action. But in reality, what truly takes place after resolutions are made?

At the beginning of the year, gyms are full of people who have made the resolution of losing weight as a top priority. Within a few months memberships are cancelled because people don't follow through.

Losing weight is just one example of a declaration for a new way of being.

What really happens when the newness of anything wears off? If there is no real conviction, no real plan, no real strategy for change, it doesn't happen!

Many people have plans and strategies but still fall short.

Real transformation takes the cooperation of the whole person engaging mind, body, and spirit. Ultimate change happens when all three are harmoniously working together.

After the celebration is over and the resolutions have been made, what real actions will you take to a new dynamic path?

365 Days to Authenticity offers you a way to create real change. There are no gimmicks. This guide is just a straight forward approach to you engaging in producing healthy practices that can bring about lasting change. This journey is about reclaiming who you really are, instead of just proclaiming something new. You will actively be transforming by letting go of what is no longer useful in your life. This is the year for paradigm shifting.

Some of the changes taking place will be simply looking at old things in a new way. Other adjustments will be life changing as you alter methods and practices to your life. New ways of thinking will change your behaviors. When new behaviors and practices are added life can progress into a dynamic path. Every month I will provide emphasis on what to work on, so by the end of the year you will have learned and implemented new skills and practices.

First Step:

Time to take inventory of your life! The great assessment! This part sounds intimidating, but it really isn't. It is the most necessary step because by taking a life assessment you become clear. When you take the time to write things down in black and white life takes on a whole new meaning. You are important and the way you function is your life statement. Business people forecast, plan, execute, and at the end of the year cut their losses. People from all walks of life re vamp, reorganize, and adjust their planning to get maximum results. You can too. It doesn't require a lot of money. The requirement involves you making a commitment to yourself to pursue a better life and engage in healthy living.

In my life coaching business, I often ask people if their life was a book and it had four chapters, what would be the name of the chapters. The first chapter represents the past. The second and third chapters represent the progressive stages of life leading to the fourth chapter. The fourth chapter is your present life.

For some people the chapters were humorous. For others the titles were bitter sweet. Many people mentioned their past and how they would make some better decisions today. Like all of us, there were some regrets. But what if you could edit chapter four, your present chapter? It sounds intriguing doesn't it? Let's start with.

What titles would you use to describe the past to your present? Whatever your reaction might be this is the start of something real and life changing for you. Name your chapters. Write them down. This is an important step because it will bring focus and clarity to what you perceive your life to be. The names you give these titles will be the basis of your work this coming year. You will not focus on your past. You will look back only for the purpose of creating a dynamic present, and ultimately your future.

The past can't be changed but when you write it down in bold black and white it will illustrate how far you have really progressed in your life already. Looking life straight in the eye is a powerful and beautiful thing. Chapters two and three are about the progression over time in your life that led you to your present. Chapter four is symbolic of your present where you think you are today.

The first chapter of your life will be your learning tool or your teacher. When reflecting on the past it is to be only used as a teaching guide so that you will make better decisions in your chapter four, which is your present.

Chapter four of your life will also be your starting point. You have the power to change which is discussed in chapter four of the book. Your chapter five and beyond, which is your future, can change dramatically if you are willing to do the work.

For example, I titled my chapters as follows; chapter one Innocent, chapter two Lost, chapter three Grace, chapter four Victorious.

I chose innocent as my first chapter. Because like I stated in the beginning of the book, we were a thought in God's mind and then we were born. So the first part of my life would be my arrival to earth and my childhood.

Chapter two is my early adult life. It was the time in my life when I was growing into a young woman. I experimented with life. I was trying to find myself and establish who I was as a person. But sadly along the way of self-discovery I got lost, and ended up compromising the values I had been taught. My story is a lot like that of the prodigal son in the bible. It is the story of the young man who wasted his fortune and got an epiphany when he woke up sleeping among the pigs.

Chapter three has been entitled Grace. Yes sweet grace! Grace is when God extended his love to me during the foolish seasons of my life. Thank God that grace and mercy is extended daily. A lot of healing took place in my life. I began to take the mistakes and experiences of my past and use them to serve others.

Chapter four is entitled Victorious! Victorious is simply overcoming my obstacles, while embracing and accepting the fullness of who I am through the power of the Holy Spirit. It doesn't mean a life without mistakes. Rather this present chapter means I am seasoned, humble, and determined to continue living a life of substance and meaning. This present chapter of my life is about learning, serving, and staying close to God. By staying close to God, the truth of who I am will continue to unfold throughout my life.

So take some time to think about your life write those chapters down but leave room for your present chapter, chapter four. As you begin to move through the book's chapters you will actually be writing and living your chapter four.

1) Writing down what isn't working in your life anymore is the first step. Being clear and honest is so essential. This is a process but remember to be gentle with yourself as things began to unfold. The list might surprise you!

2) There is so much freedom in being honest. Also there is a new accountability. Becoming clear by writing things down will allow you to see in black and white what adjustments that need to be made in your life.

Warning it is normal to feel uncomfortable during this process. But it is just a process. "This too shall pass."

A) Write down what can be salvaged, and what needs to be eliminated. These are the references to chapter two and three of your life. You have developed over time some awesome skills. But what do you currently need to let go of so that your present and future chapters can be more powerful?

Be honest, this is the getting real part. Looking back could be painful but necessary. There is a purpose for looking back. The purpose in this case is to get to the root and create a new beginning.

But be kind to yourself, this is a courageous exercise. This practice is life changing. You have truly reached a place where you are serious about how you are going to spend the rest of your life. You are choosing a better way for yourself. So allow the tears to flow as you reflect upon the powerful life you have lived to the present. How incredible is that? The great news is the way you can edit the past is by making better decisions that will make an impact on your present life. When you are conscious of your life in the present tense it will assist you with moving toward your future. You will be writing your chapters five and beyond. So stay focused.

By taking inventory of your life you will find there are many things in your life that are worth saving. The whole purpose of this exercise is to look at your life and make the necessary adjustments. These changes are opening up new pathways. With new pathways you will have new experiences. So be relentless about it!

B) Start your list! It could be old habits, attitudes, or old ways of thinking, relationships that have affected you badly, or business practices that have not work for you in a long time. Whatever the case might be it has become an obstacle to living free.

4) Start with one thing at a time. Let that one thing resonate within you before you move on to the next. Own it, and then surrender it to God. Say it to yourself, say it out loud, and write it down. You will not allow this person, this habit, this attitude, this relationship, this way of living be an obstacle in your life anymore. You've had enough! These steps are major, and letting go could cause some anxiety.

5) But push forward. These feelings of discomfort are only temporary in comparison to being free for the rest of your life.

6) Take your time! Your life circumstances didn't happen overnight. This list can be altered. But this is your starting point to get clear with yourself by writing things down.

7) Take baby steps, grieve the loss, let go and proceed. Your spirit will feel lighter. As you advance forward seeking support from professional coaches could enhance your journey. This is a complete transformation. Some areas of your life might need more attention than others. When you are on the right track you just feel good! You will be able to accomplish more in your life! This personal evaluation is the foundation of true confidence. It is true authenticity!

Change isn't easy but you are worth it. I know that the admission of the truth in your life can feel overwhelming. Take a deep breath, close your eyes, and think how far you have come in life.

This could be a good time to just think of some situations that you have already overcome. Think about your past accomplishments. More important be proud of yourself for making the decision that this will not be just another year. Your intentions and actions will not be the same. Step by step you will make the changes you desire.

9) Practice makes perfect. For this month you will practice daily no longer participating in this behavior, relationship, attitude, or habit that has altered your life in a negative way. As you continue the practice, you will feel lighter and be able to see things more clearly.

Your mind is changing, and there is a huge transformation taking place. Methods that no longer work will be replaced by powerful new ways of being. It takes intention. It takes practice. It takes perseverance. For the first thirty days of the New Year your mind will declare it as your new reality. Remember you are creating authenticity in your life. The new behavior will become a lifestyle.

Find people who will support you. Partner with people who know about your new direction. They can help you when you feel like you want to go back. They can encourage you to keep moving forward!

"Today I will calm my mind, I will release my spirit, and stay focused on what is important in my life."

This is the greatest time to surrender to God. The act of surrendering activates God's healing power. Anytime you feel overwhelm, continue to surrender for as long as it takes. Until you experience peace. True change and transformation starts with the Lord. If you have already received Jesus as your savior then this is the perfect time to go deeper in that relationship. For those who have not received the Lord, this is an invitation to receive him and ask for his forgiveness and accept salvation. The power of the Holy Spirit will be your strength and guiding force while you are doing the practical work in this process.

Note: You are changing and physical exercise is very important. I walk every morning. This is the perfect time for me to talk to God in prayer and to listen for an answer.

Everyone is different. Find a physical activity that works for your life and just do it. It is important to find a physical release while you are going through this process. Your mind, body, and spirit will be going through profound changes. There is a shifting taking place. A physical workout will release the stress of change. This could be a good time to partner with a friend to help you stay accountable. You might ask a friend to take this journey with you. It's possible that they too are searching for true change. You might be a person whose preference is to exercise alone.

Whatever your choice of exercise may be, it is important to set yourself up to succeed. There are a million ways to bring physical activity into your life. There are exercise videos you can do in the comfort of your home, as well as community centers that offer exercise and dance classes for a minimum fee. You could partner with co-workers and walk with them during breaks, or at lunch time. Be creative and integrate a routine that will work for your lifestyle. The most important thing is to remember why you are doing what you are doing. You are engaging in becoming harmonious with mind, body and spirit. You are embarking upon a balanced and healthy lifestyle. Developing an exercise program shouldn't be stressful or unrealistic. You are creating balance, when all three components work together (mind, body and spirit) the benefits are phenomenal! This journey is more than just joining a new gym class. This is about making lifestyle adjustments so you can be a more powerful you.

During this precious time that you are creating a healthier inner life, I cannot emphasize enough the power of eating well. You will need foods that will give the body nutrition and energy. Keep in mind that eating healthy does not have to be overly expensive and without taste. But begin taking inventory of what you are eating and how much. I like food but I discovered that I could eat more if I ate the right types of food. Here are a few tips that I have learned along the way. Super foods are a modern day expression for good eating. Olive oil and Grape seed oil are excellent for cooking. Foods like beans, salmon, turkey, sardines and eggs are good for lowering cholesterol. Omega threes are found in green teas, and black teas which lower the risk of heart disease, it also helps with arthritis, memory loss and Alzheimer's disease. Almond milk and coconut milk are good with hot and cold cereals. Try to avoid sugary cereals honey could be used in hot cereals. Adding flax seed helps cleanse the digestive system and energizes the body and stimulate the brain. Black beans, and pinto beans and peanut butter are a good source of protein. Dark berries such as blue berries are good antioxidants. Dark chocolate which is good news for chocolate lovers is a good source for digestion as well. Water rejuvenates the body. Also spring and alkaline waters are good sources for flushing out toxins. Baked chicken seasoned with herbs can be a good source for less fat in the diet. Let your focus be about living healthy remember paradigm shifting. No doubt you will lose the pounds when you eat well. But eating healthy gives you the energy to do the things you love to do. It will also increase your quality of life.

This is your life, do the work! The reward and benefits that you will receive will exceed any discomfort that you may experience during your time of adjustment. You are going to feel and look incredible, those are the outer benefits. But remember the deep motivation is to engage in a transformative process that will change your life. You are taking a year's journey to bring about this change! You are discovering a more powerful you!

Remember this is your new reality. You are stepping into Finding Your Authenticity!

After self examining attitudes or habits that have been obstacles to you reaching your potential, then this is a good time to explore the root cause. Take some time out to think about these questions. What are the real reasons that I have been behaving or thinking in a way that has been causing me pain? How can I create a better way of being? This is the time to get clear with yourself so be honest. This is also a time to take accountability for your actions and your life. Even though life can throw some curve balls in our direction, how we deal with these circumstances is a key element for growth. A quick note, this is not about blaming others or even yourself. Blaming creates a delay in you finding solutions. Blaming creates obstacles and excuses for moving forward. This exercise is for clearing the pathway to create new opportunities for permanent change in your life. So be relentlessly honest with yourself. If it isn't working for you then it is definitely time for a change. Get a piece of paper and make two columns on your paper. Write down the situation, habit, relationship, behavior or issue that you have been dealing with for years. Then on the other side write the change you want in your life. Your next step is to close your eyes and see that desired thing changed in your mind. The thought of new changes will feel foreign at first. In your mind's eye see yourself in the new behavior, being different in the current relationship. See the issue no longer existing, see the problem gone. Visualize yourself practicing the new behavior. Observe how your body feels. How does your mind react? The mind could possibly try to reject your new visual, but repeat the process of seeing your new change as much as possible. Also imagine how others, especially those most familiar with you, react to this change. Know they will be surprised by this new behavior and might not trust your change of behavior at the first encounter. However the way trust is built is through consistency. Others will be able to trust this new attitude and behavior if you continue to do it. The most important thing is that by activating something new you are forming a new habit and acting in behaviors that are good for you and others. This is the beginning of the building blocks to getting YOU back. The reward of getting back to the real you is that you not only feel good, but you are also reconnecting to the authentic you. There is something about living in integrity that brings you peace, which leads to confidence. When you adopt an attitude or behavior that is foreign to your nature it is an uncomfortable fit. There is a weight and a price to pay. When you make the adjustment it feels like slipping into your favorite pair of jeans. It feels totally comfortable like a second skin. With great results you're motivated to continue. Remember by continuing to practice this new behavior and attitude you are building your lifestyle change. Practice makes perfect! You are creating your new reality. Good Job! So let's continue to move forward.

If there is a relationship that has caused you a great deal of emotional pain, then it's time to look at why! The body and mind always tell us when something is wrong. Trust what your spirit is saying to you. The practical natural world reveals itself in the form of headaches, backaches, heartaches, etc. When we are moving in the wrong direction we get all kinds of signs. Deep inside we feel uneasy. Many of us try to ignore it, but the pain doesn't go away. A lot of us have resigned to living with chronic dull pain. As if this is truly the way to live.

Relationships can be complicated, and believe me I am no relationship expert. I have had my share of bad relationships. But when I took the time to thoroughly look at my relationships that were not satisfying, everything pointed back to authentic living. I had to admit to myself that the people I had chosen reflected what I really felt about myself deep down inside. We all want to be loved, but the key here is "choice". What and who had I chosen in my life? More importantly why had I chosen people who ultimately hurt me? It was a harsh revelation when I understood that I was not truly being myself. After admitting this I got busy working on reconnecting back to the path of authenticity. I had to learn true self-love. I am not talking about the vain and hollow love that's proclaimed in today's society. I am referring to the kind of love that heals, accepts, and teaches respect. I am speaking about God's unconditional love. When I really began looking at the way I treated myself, I soon got to the root of my problems and life for me began to slowly change. It is a powerful step to take accountability. It is empowering to understand that you are created out of love for the purpose to love and be loved. When you're not honoring that basic premise, you are dishonoring God, yourself, and your original intent.

So I began to search and ask myself some real tough questions about the way I was living my life. A lot of the questions were simple basic but profound. Mind, body, and spirit are all connected so if these three are out of sync so are we. I started the journey. This was my starting point.

Was I eating right, getting enough sleep, and exercising? Was I expecting someone else to do for me what I wasn't doing for myself? Was I accepting a minimal life and waiting for someone else to fill in the blanks? As a result of waiting for someone to complete me, was I participating in risky and negative behaviors to get my needs meant? Was I pursuing my interest, and setting goals for myself? Did my life and relationships reflect the true me? Had my spiritual life and connection with God been put on the back burner? What I had discovered as a result of self examination was that I had been dishonest with myself and others.

I began to take an honest look at myself. Slowly, like peeling an onion, the layers begin to shed and so did the tears. I felt like a fraud. I was not taking care of myself nor being real with anyone in my life. How long had I been living like this? The answer was a long time and the results of living like this made me feel depleted.

In my early twenties I tried to please everyone, and I sabotaged myself. There was no balance in my life. By the time I hit my thirties I was thoroughly burnt out.

My thirties turned out to be my season of recognizing that I needed to get a grip on what was really important to me. I went back to school, talked to professors, and sought advice from clergy and friends. I cried out to God, and he put me back on solid ground.

The process was tough and sometimes agonizing. But the process was nothing compared to the pain of being stuck for so many years. The daily pain had lingered for many years. When I started on the path of my true authenticity, healing, and restoration took place. It is an amazing transformation when you decide to find your true self.

An unsatisfactory relationship is one example of making a life adjustment. By getting clear you can begin to let go of old practices, you are creating a new and fresh pathway. With this new direction lasting change occurs. This year you are taking the opportunity to be intentional to reach the real and beautiful you. This step is amazing!

Taking one step at a time is the road to recovery.

Many wonderful things begin to happen. You realize that living authentically gives you peace of mind. It is an inside job. You cannot fool the universe and God. Although you may be able to fool others and yourself, authenticity cannot be manufactured. It radiates from within your core.

Being real with yourself includes letting go of anything that has not served you or others in a positive way.

As this transformation takes place, you will notice that you are attracting some new and exciting changes. Some of the physical issues you were having will strangely go away too. (If there is true chronic pain, it is recommended that you see a physician. It is always wise to consult your doctor before you start changing your diet and doing physical exercise)

Once you make the connection that your transformation involves the total you, you will gain a new awareness of your life. You will become aware of who you choosing in your life. You will want the best people to enter your life and reflect the way you treat yourself. You will begin to attract new people and new situations. Refreshing your spirit will attract many new and powerful beginnings for you.

The important thing to do is to stay on track! Getting real requires work! Being accountable during this process helps you to take responsibility for your life. As I mentioned previously it is important to partner with people you trust and can express your true feelings to. We are living in an information based society in which there are experts in many fields. Do some investigating and tap into these resources for support. Support is necessary for you to succeed.

Your pastor could be a good start. During my time as a member at my former church the pastor offered free counseling for the members. His desire was not to see people suffer simply because they do not have the financial means to seek counseling/help. Also check for opportunities within your community. There are community counselors that offer services according to your income.

But a good friend could also provide a solid sounding board for you. Choose someone you trust and who know you well. Give this person, or people, that you trust permission to be honest with you. In fact do this with several good friends and compare notes. Do the work! Living a quality life with integrity changes your dynamics. You begin to build a stronger connection to your authentic self.

The most important thing I can remember in finding the road back to my authentic self was my renewed faith and reconnection to God. I got lost (remember my second chapter) and began to compromise my true values. Reconnecting to your authentic path is finding your way back to your original intent. It is a spiritual pathway. My road to recovery took a lot of work, faith, and prayer. But there is nothing that compares to the joy and peace you find when healing takes place in your life.

During this challenging time I can't overemphasize the power of prayer and the Word of God. (We will examine the power of words, and God's word in later chapters). Praying is just talking to God. Actually we are always in conversation with God and He is talking to us too! This ongoing conversation is your connection to the source of life as you allow the layers of old attitudes, behaviors, and thinking shed. Your navigational system is prayer. Prayer will direct you, encourage you, and keep you as you continue your path of authenticity. Prayer is just one of the powerful tools in your arsenal as you continue this most significant journey!

This crucial practice will regenerate mind, body, and spirit. This book is about making a whole connection. It isn't just about making empty declarations. It is about engaging in healthy changes for life. These practices continued over a lifetime can lead to living a dynamic life, and eliminate making resolutions at all. You will be in the constant flow of regenerating which causes you to live and be your authentic self.

Wow you had no idea that this year would take off like this! What an excellent start for the New Year! No more empty and hollow resolutions. You are working on something that's real and obtainable. This is your life and you are taking steps to implement everything that you are learning into everyday practice. Every step is real and powerful. You have positioned yourself to experience your new reality. This is the journey of *finding your authenticity* and the transformation is happening now! Be proud of yourself for taking this courageous step. Every step you're taking is leading you to a more powerful you. Warning! Your present chapter is changing and by the end of this year you will be renaming your present chapter! So continue don't give up and don't look back. There is more to come!

Note: I encourage you to take your time during these first initial steps. What you are doing is life changing. You are working toward changing old ideas, attitudes, and behaviors that you have lived with for a long time. You've already taken the first step. Through admission, you no longer want your life to be dominated by habits that have eroded your success in life. You are looking for permanent change, so you will be engaging and learning new practices. These practices are building blocks. Each month you will add something new to your practices.

As you know the beginning of anything is always fun and interesting. But the commitment and maintenance is the real work. Be kind to yourself. If you need to revisit steps go back and read the chapters. If you find yourself stuck in one place surrender to God and let him in on your issue. A lot of times I find with prayer (which we will talk about later) and admitting that I am struggling with something, I am releasing my frustration to divinity. After I release and get a good night sleep amazingly the answer or provision is there for me.

Don't worry about doing things perfectly. Perfectionism isn't the goal and it isn't obtainable. This is about getting free so you can accomplish what you want in your life. This is deep self-care, so you can honor your life.

So I am your coach during this season of your life. I hope to encourage you throughout this journey. My prayer is that you go on and do great things in your life.

Note: You have already written down the obstacle or obstacles in your life that you want to change. With visualization you practiced being able to see yourself in the new change. You have begun to explore some root causes of old behaviors. Now take this new information, and transfer it onto something larger and more visible. Get a big poster board and write down the new practices that you will be adding to your life. Now turn them into goals. Give yourself time to accomplish them, you have a year. Each month the book will introduce you to practices that will assist you while you're building your new life. I am excited for you so let's move on. Add writing down time lines for what you want to accomplish. The time line will keep you accountable. Once again for an excellent outcome be consistent, but kind to yourself as you engage in your new practices. But you don't have to be rigid. Say for instance you miss days of exercising or you stumble back to a habit you are trying to overcome just release it, forgive yourself, and continue. Hang the poster in an area so you can see it. I hang mine in my home office.

As you put your plan into action, start another board to record your progress. You can even write down dates and times on how you felt when started your journey. It will be interesting to look back over the year the different emotions you wrote down as you experienced them. This indeed can be one of the most important years of your life! Make your board creative and fun let it reflect your personality. Write meaningful phrases that will encourage you along the way. These can be quotes, from people you admire, lyrics from songs or poems that inspire you. I am a big movie person I love lines from movies. It could be your own words that you created to keep you strong or scriptures from the bible, words have power. You can cut out pictures from magazines of people who have already done what you are working on to inspire you. Celebrate along the way! You can celebrate with others or you can have quiet personal moments to acknowledge your success. I highly recommend you experience the joy of the moment. Every step you take toward improving your life is very important, so be proud of yourself. You will be able to look at your board over time to see how far you are advancing. As you read and write down your evolving transformation, the subconscious and conscious work together harmoniously. You are slowly and actively changing your life.

Let's go no excuses!

MONTH 2

February: Faith and Balance

Now faith is being sure of what we hope for and certain of what we do not see. Hebrews 1:11

Faith is truly a powerful thing, and without it transformation is impossible. Transformation is change, and faith is the fuel that you will need to continue.

Actually the ingredients are faith and perseverance. As you seek the truth about yourself, faith will keep you from not giving up!

Olympic winners are a powerful source of inspiration. They push themselves beyond the limits.

These young athletes practice for years and sacrifice daily. They train in all seasons give up time and money, and practically give up their social lives for a chance to compete. They practice when no one is watching. They persevere when on lookers are questioning why don't they just give up.

They exemplify heart, courage and stamina. Many of them won't make it to the big event. Many of the athletes do return home without any medals.

But do they think it was worth it? You bet they do. What happens to the person that moves out on faith?

An incredible sense of freedom and empowerment is the result of engaging in what you believe in.

Many of the Olympic athletes that don't medal come back four years later and do it all over again.

Faith changes you, faith changes me, and others are inspired!

My eldest son played basketball from the time when he was a young child up into his college years. I use to watch him practice and train during his off and on seasons. His practices were always intense. He spent a certain amount of time exercising and in his later years he added weights for strength. But it was the amount of time he spent on shooting the ball from different angles that was impressive, he was tireless and consistent. A lot of young players he played against "talked trash" while playing against him in his games. My son is a reserved and quiet person. I told him to use those instances of "trash talking" to his advantage. We talked about using his focus and his faith to concentrate. It worked what he practiced kicked in so his body naturally made the moves. His faith gave him the ability to tune out his opponents and score for his team. There was one game when the score was tied against a junior high team. The clock was ticking down, we have all seen those moments in movies when the intensity is heart wrenching. The clock is running down, the moment is tense. Because of my son's natural ability, practice, focus and faith, he made the last shot, and the most beautiful sound in basketball is when the ball goes in and you witness nothing but net. The most spectacular sound was the sound of swoosh as the basket ball sailed into the net. Then the buzzer sounded off signifying that the game was over. Needless to say his team won the game! One of the things that I really love about him is that he always gave God the glory, whether he won or lost.

The Olympic athletes and my son practiced focus and faith to achieve their goals. Let's look at a man in the Bible who did the same.

My youngest brother Kenneth is an associate minister residing in San Antonio Texas. At one point when I was struggling through a difficult time in my life, I called him up. During our conversation he made reference to the story of Noah in the bible. Now I knew the story of Noah. I grew up in church learning about the different biblical heroes when I was a small child. Most people know the story of Noah, being that God asked him to build an arc because rain was coming and it would flood the earth.

But my brother told me the in-depth story of Noah and as a writer the back story of anything is always interesting to me.

He said that Noah's story was about a man that did not even know what rain was, but because of his faith in God he began building the arc. That blew my mind! Belief is a powerful thing! Noah was ridiculed and laughed at but he continued. (remember focus)

By Noah stepping out on what he believed in, it gave God the space to operate in his life. There are some situations that take bold moves so we can obtain extraordinary results!

We all know the end of the story. The rain did come, and Noah, his family, and the creatures of the earth were safe and secure on the arc. (Genesis 7: 1-24)

This is a great place to talk about the power of purpose. When purpose is realized life takes on a whole new meaning. Purpose supplies the focus and the outline of a person's life.

When we are aware of the reasons that we are here we streamline our lives to be much more productive. Our daily decisions will be based upon where we are headed. This simply means we don't waste time on going in a direction that is not consistent with our reason for being.

Purpose has caused me to look at my life in a whole different way. In the past, I use to just jump at any opportunity that came my way. I just saw all opportunities as blessings. I do believe that all blessings come from the Lord. But before I understood my purpose, I use to just react. I now take my time to pray and consult God before I make a move. I make sure that the decisions that I am making are according to my purpose. Some opportunities are good, but what is the best choice according to your purpose, which is God's blue print for your life.

Remember our discussion on original intent? That everything about you has been made for your purpose in life. Something extraordinary happens when you find that path. The pieces of your life begin to fall into place. In my coaching business, *Finding Your Authentic Path*, I created an assessment entitled "Pieces to A Dream Life." This questionnaire asks questions about your life, work, personality, and dreams. The questionnaire's purpose is to bring focus to your life. It is an instrument for fine tuning, designed to get the participant to look at their natural talents and natural inclinations in life. When we get settled into who we are at the core, our decisions begin to become tailored and streamlined.

When purpose is the driving force behind our decisions the bumps and the bruises we encounter along the way seem to be worth it.

Understanding your purpose doesn't mean you have *cart blanche* to life. It doesn't mean you won't have challenges, disappointments, or even setbacks. It does mean that your life isn't just haphazard. It does mean that there is a reason why you have been born. It also means that relying upon faith is integral as you continue your journey.

Faith will keep you through the rainy seasons in life. When there is no evidence that the things you are praying for and working on is even in clear view. It can be easy to get discouraged. But when you push through, the benefits can be staggering. God charged Noah with building the Arc because mankind was not operating in his original intent. (Genesis 6: 13-14) Man was not in alignment, and we all know when something is not in alignment the use turns dysfunctional rather than functional.

Search deep within your heart, and ask yourself what God has charged you to do with your life? If it is something that has been nagging your conscious for a long time, could it be a clue to what your purpose is?

It has taken faith to step forward the way you are doing, and it will take faith to continue. The work becomes secondary when it produces powerful change.

Even after faith is ignited, the process at times can be difficult but it is also part of the process. It builds muscle, stamina, and character.

Belief sends a powerful message to the universe. One that says I am ready to take action on what I believe in.

When a person believes, actions and moving forward is implemented.

How awesome the possibilities are endless. That excites me, and I hope that you are inspired as well to keep allowing the layers of the old to shed.

Step forward and watch as the universe opens up to you! Mark: 9:39 says all things are possible for those who believe! Welcome to your real way of being. Welcome to your new reality! Welcome to your authentic path.

Note: Continue to exercise, eat well, pray, and walk in faith as you move through this process. Keep in touch with your support group. They are the people who you have chosen to assist you through your change. They are a part of your team and will help you stay accountable. If you need to revisit some steps, do so. The whole idea is to live in integrity and honesty. It builds character, courage, confidence, and releases peace in your life.

The power of balance:

You have embarked upon a powerful journey, and you are utilizing tools to help you succeed. Faith is your fuel, purpose is your direction, and balance will keep your life enriched as you travel on your authentic path.

Webster's Dictionary had several definitions of balance:

1) Noun: an even distribution of weight enabling someone or something to remain upright and steady.

2) Verb: Keep or put in a steady position so that it does not fall.

3) Mental and emotional steadiness

All of these definitions can be applied to you as you search and continue to create your new reality.

What does balance look like in your everyday life as you advance forward?

This is powerful work that you are doing. Your mind body and spirit are being challenged in new ways. This experience can be draining at times. That's why it is so important to integrate a balanced life, so this experience can be even more satisfying.

Balance in everyday living includes staying connected to life, and staying connected to the source of life, which is God. Balance is simply staying in tune not allowing yourself to live in extremes which can cause mental and physical exhaustion.

As I spoke about in the last chapter, eating the right foods keeps the body strong. Drinking water replenishes the body. While exercise and physical movement keeps your body working well. Sleep refuels and regenerates the body.

But human beings are also need time for socializing. During this time of self-care it is important to stay connected to family and friends. More importantly stay connected to your spirit, which is through God, the source of life. Listen to the spirit as it will keep you balanced.

Take time to enjoy people. This is vital and will make this experience even more pleasurable and significant.

Even as I am writing this book I am taking calls from friends and catching up. I am grateful to be able to take the time to pursue my writing. Two years ago, my schedule was extremely hectic due to my work as a social worker, and various family obligations. When my mother got really sick I had to decide if I was going to continue to help my siblings take care of our mother, while maintaining my very stressful job. After much prayer, I transitioned into my life coaching business. I am still committed to my work, but my schedule is more flexible.

Writing this book is a part of balancing my time. Writing is a solo venture. Writers spend enormous amounts of time in solitude. The writing process demands time to think, process, create, and execute.

So it is vital to stay active. Sometimes I have to get out of my own head. I walk in the mornings, either on my treadmill or a trail near my house. I prefer walking the trail in the early mornings because I get the chance to commune with nature and talk to God. It is a wonderful experience. If the weather doesn't permit, I have a treadmill in my home office. It's a bit more challenging to exercise on the treadmill. I prefer being outside, but it's a backup plan when the weather isn't favorable. I also enjoy working in my very small make shift garden. It is amazing to see things grow. But these activities are also solo. So I try to balance work and social aspects in order to stay connected.

Part of balancing my time also includes seeing clients. I have to pay the bills, so I do what I love in the early morning, the writing. Then I continue to do what I love in the early afternoon and that's life coaching.

Note: I haven't always lived a balanced life, and I am still challenged daily to live in balance. But I am learning to listen to my spirit and be intentional with my time. Meaning I need to be disciplined to get task done, but I also need to take time to be spontaneous so I can live in the present.

As mentioned previously a few years ago my life changed dramatically when my parents passed away. I was experiencing exhaustion from working long hours on my job and helping my family care for our parents. I had to make a decision so that I could have quality of life while my parents were going through their last stage of life.

I resigned from my job, took a small pension, and transferred my skills to my life coaching business. I have to admit the money has been a challenge, but the peace from that decision is priceless. It's up to each person how he or she will proceed with the rest of their life. But if you find yourself not satisfied and constantly tired, it could be the time to pull back and make some life decisions that will position you for your desired life.

Normally in the late afternoon is when my schedule permits the time to connect with my family or friends. Writing in the mornings is perfect for me because that's my high energy time. It's the most creative time for me. That's when the spirit of God downloads into my spirit. I am listening so I can manifest it in my life.

Note: It's really important to examine when your high energy time is. I ask this question in my Pieces to a Dream Life questionnaire. What time of day does your natural energy flow? Some people are nocturnal; they do well in the evenings and late at night. Others are morning people they do well in early mornings. Be aware of that fuse of energy. That's the time to maximize your productivity. Tailoring your life to who you already are is a fun adventure. When you find that, you create more peace in your life.

Everyone's reality is different. The 21st century person has multiple obligations. But a life out of balance comes with a price. Extreme living has affected our balance. Many of us are burnt out or exhausted most of the time. When we are tired all of the time there is no room for creativity, fun, or living. Living in extremes can cause physical and mental health issues. Living out of balance slowly erodes energy. The modern day life can be compared to that of a juggler. We all know what happens when you have one too many balls in the air. They come crashing down.

The most important thing is to tailor your life so you can live in balance. By actually scheduling times around your work, you will be able to have time for living. Work takes a huge chunk of our time. Work is one of life's necessities so we can maintain our life. It can't be our total focus, because then we would neglect the reason why we're working. Work is a good and honorable thing. We need to work to take care of our lives. But when work becomes the center of our lives it causes imbalance. Work wasn't designed to fulfill all of our needs. In today's manic society, people now are measured by the amount of hours they clock in daily. It's as if we wear our work hours as a badge of honor. Finding your true self includes doing the work that you were created to do. Your work is your gift to the world. But it's just one aspect and one dimension of life. Allowing work to become the center of your life causes negative effects which result in extreme living. When we live in extremes we lose ourselves, and we actually become ineffective. It steals our joy! Living a balanced life protects us from developing negative life styles. In other words it keeps us from living in unhealthy ways.

Balance is like a great meal. You taste all those wonderful ingredients blended together, and it brings delicious flavor to a meal. Balance is the flavor of life. So take the time to integrate family, work, play, friends, interest, goals, and purpose. Life becomes much more fulfilling and truly successful!

Review in month 1: You took inventory and practiced the art of letting go: you reflected on your life chapters: old habits, thoughts, attitudes, or relationships that no longer serve your present life. I call this the art of Surrender! You experienced freedom from the old and obsolete.

Review in month 2: You continued the practice of letting go, no longer being bound to experiences, habits, relationships, and attitudes that robbed you of being your authentic self. You acknowledged that true transformation takes place when you yield to Jesus by receiving him as your Lord and Savior. Or if you have already received Him, you repositioned your life by developing a deeper commitment to honor him by living authentically. It took courage to look at your life, and acknowledge the changes that needed to be made. Prayer is your navigational system and you are standing firm! You are walking in faith and practicing balance. You are becoming conscious of the decisions you are making, and how they affect your life. You are also evaluating your purpose and analyzing if the decisions you are making are according to your purpose.

You have acquired new skills. The power to take control and the power of letting go is the perfect balance. The assessment and inventory was taken to redefine your life! If there was something to salvage, a relationship or a way of thinking, then you took the necessary steps. If you discovered after taking your assessment the relationships, habits, attitudes that caused you pain you surrendered it to God. There now is a balance between taking control when necessary, and letting go. This new skill is now a part of your personal growth to live closer to the true and real you.

As you continue this journey build upon what you are learning. Nourish the mind with the word of God. Feed the spirit with prayer. Rejuvenate the body with eating healthy and exercise until these practices become a part of your new reality.

While you are experiencing profound changes in your life, continue to practice your new lifestyle as you add and learn new skills from the up and coming chapters in the book. Transformation is a process, but it takes discipline and intentional actions in your day to day living to make this your new reality.

The assessment was your starting point. Every thirty days you will integrate information into your new found practices. The idea is to create permanent and lasting change. So be encouraged, and revisit any step as much as necessary to reclaim your new path!

MONTH 3

March: Letting go and living in the present

Now that you have taken inventory of your life in the first and second month, in the third month you will continue the practice of letting go by living in the present. Living in the present helps you to focus on the now. Part of letting go is no longer allowing anxious thoughts and behaviors dominate your life. Living in the present will assist you with fully experiencing your life. This practice will heighten your sensory experiences, and help you to relax and have authentic moments. Living in the present gives you the opportunity and pleasure of just being. Living in the present accelerates the power of living with quality. It slows things down. You are engaging in the now. It will open you up, and it will help you celebrate life now! These are a few exercises that will help you maximize present living.

1) Stop, listen, and look into the eyes of the person you are talking to. Listen to them. Don't just wait to interject the next sentence. Train your mind to be right there, this is life changing. The person you are talking to will feel supported, and you will feel gratitude to have engaged in that real moment.

2) Take time to pause during the day. Don't do anything during this time to get things done, just take pauses, it will enhance your productivity.

3) Give in to that moment. Take time to enjoy your meal without reading something. Or just read something, pause, and let the information resonate before you continue on.

4) If you are with people, don't think about what is coming next enjoy the experience.

5) If you are alone experience the sounds around you. If you are outside let nature speak to you. Whenever you go to a busy restaurant, listen to the music and sounds of activity around you. The orchestration of what it takes to get the food to the people.

6) When you are hurried, and feeling out of balance, find a quiet place and close your eyes. Let the silence wash over you.

"Be Still And Know I Am God."(Psalm 46:10)

7) Hone in on what you are engaging in, whether you are alone or with people. Let your sensory perception flow into what you are experiencing. Children do it all the time. They play and enjoy the moment.

8) Living in the present increases your focus and the quality of your life experience. You are not rushing to get to the next thing. You are there, and your subconscious is taking snap shots so your memory will have pleasurable moments.

9) You will be able to recall it later. The now is extracting everything out of that experience. It will assist you in becoming attentive to detail. It will also increase your gratitude. You will experience the joy of being alive.

Social media can be used for so many positive things. It is a window to the world. Instead of waiting for hours or days to communicate with someone across the world, this can now be done in seconds. However people are now interrupting precious moments by the excessive use of the click of the camera on their phones and posting that information. I know there are moments in life when recording special moments will give joy instantly. All of us have photographs that capture priceless memories. But when we are obsessive with taking pictures of every experience, we are interrupting the moment. If we are out and overly involved with our telephones, we miss what's happening around us. Now the people that know me well know that I struggle with using most technological devices. This is not to put a damper on those who are quite efficient and enjoy all the new gadgets of our times. This is just a statement about being in the now, and spending time while the experience is happening to be more than enough. At best, life is a collection of moments. Just stand and be still and allow that moment to wash over you. When we rush through life we miss it. So stay aware of the now!

Now you have added a new consciousness to what you have already learned. You are building and executing this new found knowledge. Continue to stay consistent. Review the life chapters you named, and look at your present chapter. Life is slowly and progressively changing for you. It feels great! The change is affecting every aspect of your life mind, body and soul.

MONTH 4

April: The Power of meditation and Prayer

I will allow my mind to become free. Meditation and prayer will become my everyday practice. This practice is a part of moving forward to an authentic life.

There is power in being still and letting your mind rest. For some people this could present a challenge. I hear people saying all the time "I don't have time for this" or "I am too busy". That's my point exactly. Some of our schedules are so crowded, and our exhaustion is profound. Most people these days just fall into bed after a busy day and the next day start all over again.

I actually believe that meditation can cause you to be more productive, while prayer keeps God in the active process of your daily connection to him. I don't mean to add more to your schedule. But in the silence of the mind, one can become more efficient. Is it possible that while you're mind is at ease answers effortlessly comes? Some of the stuff that we pollute our minds with will naturally be released. The act of letting go gives divinity a chance to nurture you. We all need restoring because of this crazy and busy world we live in.

Meditation gives us time to reconnect to our spirit, and to listen to our souls.

When the mind and body are relaxed, thinking becomes clear. Suddenly you might discover the answer to a problem. Or at a given moment you may know how to proceed with a decision that has been nagging your thoughts. Quieting the mind gives you a chance to get in touch with your spirit. The core essence of your being. With this practice you will stay in tune to your true existence. It will keep you peaceful and in tune to what is important to you.

Note: At first this practice will appear uncomfortable and random thoughts will just go crazy in your mind. But stay in the silence, and soon you will surrender the control and peace will come. First find a comfortable place. Then make sure you have comfortable clothing on. You can sit on the floor with pillows, or a comfortable chair. Close your eyes, so you can shut out the world. Some people prefer music. But some people like complete silence. Start off with 5- 7 minutes and then increase your time. Some of us are morning people. I like to meditate early in the morning when everything is quiet. I get profound answers and instructions for my day. It also gives me time to day dream. Many times those day dreams have manifested in my life. This is my time to be one with God. This is my time of prayer and listening. This is my time to meditate upon the word of God.(But his delight is in the law of the Lord and in His law he mediates day and night. Psalm 1:2)

Some people are more awake in the latter part of the day. If this is you, take the time to set aside time and practice. It could give you more resiliency and focus throughout your work day.

The power of prayer has no limits. Prayer is making your request to God. It is your connection to divinity. Prayer is the ingredient that moves the heart of God. When the heart of God has been moved, change occurs. When you allow the mind to relax it opens space for the word of God to enter into the conscious. God is always speaking. But because of the extreme activity in modern culture, we cannot hear. Prayer is the open conversation between man and God. Meditation is the receiver to hear your highest solution to your situation. When we read the Word of God, meditate upon his word, and pray, we become the conduit for bringing change to the earth. Transformation is the result. Your world changes the environment you are in changes as well. This is what your journey of authentic living is about, empowering, stepping out on what you believe in to change your world.

Review: You have acquired new skills: You have learned the art of living in the present by capturing the moment, being conscious, and living in the now. It has heightened your sensory experience. It produces more joy and you are able to experience more gratitude. You are grateful for being alive.

Now you are adding the power of meditation and prayer which is the art of being still while acknowledging your connection with the spirit of God! You have seasoned this practice with the word of God. This practice is the fabric of your permanent change. You are taking time to honor the life you have been given. In this peace you will find revelation, efficiency, focus and so much more. Now add all of these new skills and practices to your life. This is your new reality. You are walking in your authentic path.

MONTH 5

May: In this month you will practice the art of forgiveness.

This practice will lead to healing old wounds, the forgiveness of others, and more importantly the forgiveness of self. Yes, the forgiving of self is just as important as forgiving others. It releases you from past mistakes. By practicing forgiveness you are experiencing love on the highest level. This practice will keep your heart and mind clear, and refresh your spirit. In this practice, humility and grace will adopt you and an inner beauty can operate from the inside.

Many people do understand the significance of forgiving others. Forgiveness allows the circumstance or person to no longer have control in your life. The letting go expands your capacity to love.

This process of taking inventory of your life is letting go and allowing these changes to transform you. I think the continued practice of forgiveness is vital in regenerating life. Unforgivenss can cause some serious spiritual, physical, and mental health issues. The mind, body, and spirit are always working in conjunction or in dysfunction with each other.

There are different opinions about if unforgiveness can aggravate or cause disease. But these are my thoughts. When unforgiveness occurs some of the emotions that can be experienced is anger, frustration, resentment and hurt. Imagine feeling those emotions and carrying those emotions around when you think of a person. This example reminds me of holding your breath and exhaling. You can only hold your breath for a certain length of time without becoming uncomfortable. When you release your lungs are full of oxygen again. You feel normal again and comfortable. Holding on to unforgivness is painful and it's like a sore that doesn't heal. There is no disconnection between your thoughts, emotions and your body. Try thinking of something pleasant and observe how you feel and your body feels. Now think of something unpleasant or painful once again observe how you feel emotionally and how your body feels. Holding on to negative emotions causes different responses in the body. Holding on to negative emotions for years has to cause damage to the body in some way. Ancient cultures like Asian, African, and Native Americans understand the connection between mind, body, and spirit. Although

Western culture is catching up and making advances to this way of thinking, still more needs to be done. In general being upset with someone for a long period of time and not letting go, holds you in captivity. It controls you. That person may not know that you are upset, or maybe the act was intentional. To replay the act over and over again erodes the mind. Ironically we all want forgiveness, we all want mercy. Jesus said to forgive your brother not 7 times, but seventy times seven (Mathew 18:22). That's a whole lot of forgiveness! The idea is to forgive, and receive peace of mind and an open heart.

Forgiveness for many is a process. Forgiveness can be one of the most challenging things to do in life. Even though we understand intellectually that we need to forgive, it can be very hard to deal with because of the hurt that we experience. Forgiveness is a spiritual thing. It has to be dealt with from the heart. Even though our conscious mind is aware, even though we say it out loud, it is the heart that has to be clear. Forgiveness is the provision that God made so we can reconnect and make a new start.

I grew up in a tough environment but my parents provided all the material things that our family needed. My mother was a genius when it came to making our family feel like we were rich. My father worked very hard to provide for our family. Looking back over his background he encountered extreme discrimination as a young African American boy growing up in the South. He also came from a very strict religious family culture, and he left home at a very early age. My father was a very young man and he learned about life through his encounters from street mentors.

Through my dad's decision to leave home at an early age, he learned how to become a man through trial and error. When facing the pressures of life he chose drinking as his way of coping.

Even with conflicts and contradictions in his life, he served in the military. I didn't know until his passing that he had received medals of Honor. My father received several decorative medals while serving in the US Army. He received the World War II Victory Medal, American Campaign Medal, Good Conduct Medal, European-African Medal and 4 Bronze Stars.

He, among many men of his time, developed PTSD (post-traumatic stress disorder). A lot of war veterans have suffered with this syndrome following the after math of war. They relive some of the casualties of their war experiences, even after returning home. But during my father's time a lot of men dealt with PTSD and moved on in their life without treatment. Today PTSD is understood and treated. At the time my family didn't have this knowledge. As my father's drinking escalated over time we suffered as a family through his fits of anger. The scars ran deep, and it profoundly changed me and my siblings' lives. In the latter years of his life he was diagnose and treated for PTSD.

I took steps, and I released the pain of not forgiving my father over time to God. Living in an emotional state of unforgiveness held me in captivity for years. Over the years, consciously letting go allowed me to have a better relationship with my father and to be at peace with myself.

Over time my father gave up drinking. Those were the years I got to know him as a person, not just my father. While he was drinking, he was a talkative charismatic man. But in reality he was a quiet man with simple taste.

He was an excellent storyteller. I enjoyed his stories about places he saw while serving in the military during World War II. I discovered from my father's stories why I have such an obsession with Paris. He spoke fondly of his experiences he had in Italy, France, and Germany.

My dad also could tell a good joke. He wore a poker face when telling his jokes, always looking at the listener to see their reaction. He had a good laugh after leading the person to the punch line.

In his last years on the earth I was able to experience him as a very caring and sweet man. I enjoyed those last days very much. Sometimes he would call me and say "I would like to have a burger with no onions and cheese". There were times when I would be in the middle of doing something, but I would respond and say "give me a little time and I will be right over". Sharing a hamburger while hearing one of his many stories, were some of the most precious times we shared.

Forgiving my father over time and understanding the root of his problems, led me to my life's work. It also led me to a healthy relationship with him. What I experienced growing up led me to become a social worker, teacher, and life coach. I taught children who were living in high risk areas and worked with families who were in domestic violence. I also worked for a foundation to find homes for abused and neglected children. Today I teach a forgiveness class at a local domestic violence shelter. I wanted to offer the families more than just another motivational class. My purpose is for the women to let go of the past events in their lives by acknowledging the pain and lost, but start fresh. This is no easy situation. Many of the women have been in the shelter for weeks, and others had just escaped violence. The way I set it up is, I have three colorful bags. They are entitled forgiveness of people who have hurt me, forgiveness of self, and others who need to forgive me. I also have a huge jar with the words paid in full written on it. I ask the women to write down any person that would fit into the three bags. They then put the names of the people in the bags. This is done strictly on a volunteer basis. There have been women who said they were not willing to forgive past or present people who caused violence against them. Many couldn't forgive themselves as well. But there were some who could forgive and wrote names for all of the bags. Those are the ones that I poured their names into the large jar that said paid in full. I explained to them that the act of forgiveness is like a debt that has been paid in full. I offer them candy and invited them to taste the sweet taste of life. For the women who decided not to release any names of people in all of the bags, I offered them dill pickles. Although the pickles are fresh and good, it symbolizes still some hurt and bitterness that they had not overcome yet. Some of the women could forgive some people who had hurt them but not all, so they were asked to take pickles, and candy representing the bitter sweet taste of life. This demonstration opened up discussions about some painful past and present events that the women had experienced. At the end of all sessions I take the names and don't read them. I burn all of the names (later in my kitchen sink at home) in agreement with the ladies, the past is now ashes. This exercise alone is powerful. Some participate and express their pain and some just listen and cry in silence. This class is held every three weeks for an hour. Within a three week time frame many of the women move on, some of the faces are familiar. Along with my forgiveness bags and debt paid in full jar, we have discussions about how unforgiveness and forgiveness can affect the mind body and spirit. Many of the women suffer from physical issues. There is a discussion on how unforgiveness might not be the cause of certain diseases but how the lack of letting go harmful emotions can negatively affect the body. I try to make sure the information I am sharing is powerful because many would be moving on. For the ones who have a longer stay, I want the class to remain fresh. I encourage the women to use their time wisely and to develop a good relationship with their social workers to use all the resources that are available to them. At the end of each class, there are written affirmations that I have written out and if they choose they can take with them. Now the rule of the shelter is not to preach your faith to the women. The women have the freedom to attend church or not. The shelter provides outlets for the women to worship, if they chose. But I always let the women know that I am a believer of Jesus Christ, and I believe that his death on the cross was the ultimate act of forgiveness. The beauty of being able to serve the women is that I get to meet a diverse cross section of women. I am able to use my skills as a former social worker to assist them. At the end of the hour I always ask if anyone would like prayer. There are some who are angry with God and I am very respectful of where they are, and their belief system. Interestingly a lot of the women do want prayer. This class is not only for the women but it's for me as well. It keeps me centered and clear. I always self examine if there is any unforgivenss in my life. I can't teach the class if I don't live it.

Forgiveness can untie God's hands. Forgiving can create a powerful future for the person who is willing to pardon and let go of someone's past offenses.

Last but not least forgiving yourself can be the ultimate challenge for most of us. Just like forgiving others, forgiving your self is equally important. A lot of us are very hard on ourselves. The process of taking inventory of your life has given you insight into perhaps some gross mistakes that you have made. All of us have been hurt, but don't forget there are people who need to forgive us too. Whether it has been intentional or unintentional, at some point in time we have hurt others. It is important to go to that person, if possible, and ask for forgiveness. If that person has already passed, we can surrender that hurt and guilt to God. Along with hurting others, some of us haven't been that great to ourselves. It is so important to accept yourself. You are currently working on improving your life. Some people spend a lot of time worrying about their past mistakes. This realization can cause much suffering. Don't spend any more time, present or future, worrying about what has been lost. That includes time and money that has been spent as well. The point is you can never get that back! It's gone, it's over! The past can be utilized as a teacher. The knowledge of the past can be used to create a better present and future life. Forgiving yourself is learning how to love and accept yourself. It creates healing and a healthier pathway to living. Forgiveness is the washing of the soul. Letting go creates spiritual, mental, and physical space to be filled with something new. That's what this year is about, creating something new in your life. This is the practice and celebration of your new reality.

Note: Forgiveness will give you more energy. Caution you can begin to feel really light, free, and peaceful! Continue to enhance your being with healthy foods, water, prayer, exercise, meditation, and good sleep. You are doing well! Now let's press forward and continue on this magnificent journey!

MONTH 6

June: The discarding of old things

As you are moving into creating new space in your heart your physical space should reflect that too. This month is the practice of getting rid of old things in your office, home, or whatever space you spend a lot of time. The idea is to streamline and organize your life. In the previous chapters, you focused on clearing the mind and freeing your spirit. Now let your physical space reflect that as well. Like I mentioned in the earlier chapters everything doesn't need to be thrown out. You might be able to salvage or repurpose some of your possessions. You and I both know there are items in our home or office that are just taking up space and you haven't used them in a long time.

Start like you started in the beginning of the book by taking inventory. This could be done on a Saturday or a off day, when you have time. Actually it doesn't have to be done all in one weekend, but spend the next thirty days going through this process until you see some real progress.

1) Start in one room at a time. You can start in your bedroom. Okay we all have articles of clothing that we haven't worn in years. If you are anything like me, your intention is to save an article of clothing until "I am able to lose the weight". Now this is an admirable thing to do. But could there be other reasons, such as.

a) You invested some good money in it, and can't stand to let that item go, even though you don't wear it.

b) You just haven't gotten around to doing anything with it over time.

The answer could be a, or b, or both. In any case you are here and you have made the decision to act, to do something. Congratulations this is a very good thing.

Okay now that we are clear, we will start the process. You will need:

1) Three boxes, a large black marker, tape, and some white paper.

2) On each of the boxes you are going to label:

a) Recovery
b) Give away
c) Throw away

Now put on your favorite music, and make sure you have a couple bottles of water near. Put on some comfortable clothes, and go to work.

Your recovery box is for clothing that you know you are going to wear, but they are in need of repair. With these clothes you will either make repairs or take them to the cleaners. Some people prefer to mend their own clothing, but some might prefer to just take them to a local cleaner and let them do the repairs. According to your budget and time this is a personal choice. In any case you are moving forward.

Now be honest with your recovery box. If it is items of clothing that you know you are really not going to wear again, even if you get them repaired, put those items in your give away box. Now I know this will be a challenge for some. We all have clothing that we have an emotional attachment to. But the point of this exercise, like this entire year, is to take inventory and to make necessary life adjustments. So with that being said, keep moving, you are getting there!

The giveaway box is a special box. This box symbolizes letting go. But the letting go will benefit others. There are many organizations that will take used clothing to help people in need. There are domestic violent shelters with women who had to leave their homes immediately, taking their children with little to no clothing at all. They had to find safe shelters in order to get away from a violent situation. These women, in many cases have to start their lives over, with minimum resources. Donating clothing to a domestic violent shelter in your city could be a real blessing to families as well.

There are other organizations where donations would be appreciated, such as women getting their lives together after being incarcerated. Many times these ladies need appropriate attire to wear when searching for employment. The homeless population is also a good place to donate. Some people are desperately trying to get their lives back, and clothing could make a huge difference. Also check out organizations that will come to your home to pick up items that you no longer use.

Do some investigating in your community to find out where you would like to contribute, and do it.

Now the last box is the throw away box. This box is for clothing that has gone way beyond repair. We have clothes and shoes that we know for sure there is no help for these pitiful things, and we just need to get rid of these items.

The truth of the matter is that a lot of things we don't really use have worn out their purpose. There are so many reasons why, we all have busy lives, but now this process is helping us to focus on doing something about it.

This exercise of recovery, giving away, and throwing away is part of the process of making adjustments to your life. Repeat this process in other areas of your living space. Have a garage sale. Get a friend to help you organize your things, put a sign out on your lawn, and do it on a Saturday morning. You can make a small profit and use the money to take a friend to lunch, put it in savings, or donate the cash. Whatever you decide to do, it turns out to be a win-win situation.

Do this process for thirty days until every area of your home, office, or apartment is clutter free. The mental and spiritual benefits from doing this practice are priceless. Now in order to stay clutter free, do this practice periodically. Because remember, this is the year of transformation. This is your new reality.

Review: You have acquired new life skills. You practiced the art of forgiveness, which is really the highest act of love. You've practice forgiving others and forgiving yourself.

Next you de-cluttered your physical space. In the process you were able to give to others, and help people in your community who were in need. Just by giving away the things you no longer needed, you were able to make a huge difference in others life. How wonderful. Last you were able to make a little extra cash by getting rid of some items in your garage.

This exercise, like the exercise in the beginning of the book is expanding your world. You are opening up your life to new pathways. You are opening up your life to abundance, by giving and letting go.

Note: There is so much freedom in giving, it creates the perfect balance. In giving you receive peace to your soul. There is no amount of money on earth that can give you that kind of peace. In your giving you shall receive.

MONTH 7

July: The Art of doing something new!

This practice is the most adventurous one. But for many this could be the most challenging exercise. For the next thirty days you will be doing things for the first time. These exercises are to bring into your life a fresh and bold path. Yes it can be intimidating! Most of us live in our comfort zones.

We have found our niches, and in a lot of cases these are the same routines that have us feeling lethargic and stuck. This is the month to do something different. Once a week for the next 30 days, which means four different activities, you will do something new. It may be something you have wanted to do all of your life, but just haven't made it happen yet. Take small steps. It doesn't have to be something big like jumping out of a plane. Although this could be perfect for someone who just need to really get out of a rut. This is a personal choice. It could be something simple and different to get out of the familiar.

About three years ago I embarked upon a journey to do things that I have never done before. At the time my youngest son moved back home and he was interested in trying some new things too. Exploring new things open up my creativity. We went to some cultural things in my city. At the time he was dating a young woman who was pursuing photography. I wanted to take a family picture with both of my sons. But I wanted something different than just the studio type picture. So we decided our location would be in Red Rock Canyon (location in Las Vegas). We decided to dress in white, linen like clothing. We also gathered props from the house, a gourd with orange calla lilies and an African style seat. This was very different for all of us. It was in the spring time in Las Vegas and the temperatures were quite warm. So we took bottled water and trail mix, to keep from getting dehydrated and to keep our energy going. It was a fun adventure. The photographer brought her young daughter and she got to play and enjoy herself. The shoot attracted a lot of curious on lookers, and of course we hammed it up. The pictures were absolutely gorgeous she really captured the spirit of our family. The experience was exhilarating we all had dinner that evening at my house. That event assisted me with expanding my creativity. Suddenly doors that I was afraid to walk through for years flung open! I took an interior design class and met a woman who turned out to be a good friend. We went to openings at high end furniture stores. We also traveled together. We attended ABFF Film Festival in Miami (American Black Film Festival) The experience was electric and interesting watching young film makers gather together to learn from masters and pitch their films. As a result I wrote my first screenplay, (it hasn't been sold yet, but it is copy written under the Writer's Guild of America "entitled Full Circle) Expressing myself creatively took me to new levels. I finally had the courage to allow my artistic side to flourish.

My youngest son also continued to do some creative outings with me. One time we had high tea at the Ritz Carlton it felt totally luxurious. The dining room was elegant with polished silverware and linen table cloths. We were seated near French doors so we could see the beautiful garden. The assortment of teas with their exotic smells made us feel like we had been transported to another country. We had just started learning how to play chess, and we took our chess board with us. It was a wonderful time to experience something new, while learning something new. The time spent with my son was invaluable.

Another creative thing that we did was go to an international chess tournament at the MGM Grand Hotel in Las Vegas. The price was inexpensive to get in, so we went to observe the masters. What I really loved about the tournament was the cross section of people. This event attracted young and old, men and women, and people of different nationalities. The commonality was the game. It was very inspiring. My son actually became very skilled at chess, and I am still a novice. Being skilled was less of a goal for me than trying something different. Learning something new or doing something new makes life more interesting. My son now plays chess wherever he travels, and he has met some interesting players along the way. By the way, I am sharing my experiences. Everyone is different. Some of the things that I suggested could be something you would like to try or just too far over the moon for you. But this chapter is about doing something new. So create your own new thing according to your time, interest, and finances.

For the next thirty days, which might be easier to do on weekends, you will engage in new activities at least four times. Discover your city in a new and different way. Find four activities or interest that you could do. If you don't want to do it alone, get a friend or two to sign up. Remember the friends and support group discussed in the earlier chapters. This could be a fun and a new thing for you and your friends. Remember to keep in mind your growth. This is about your expansion. You possibly could meet new people, and develop new friendships. Starting something new has taken my life to an artistic direction that has given me deep fulfillment. I'll just say this, seeking out new things refreshes life and adds new dimensions. When I went to Barcelona (which I will talk about dream trips later) me and my companions visited the Picasso Museum of Art. Picasso is one of my favorite artist. The first room displayed his early etchings as a young boy. In each room we saw how he matured over time as an artist. He painted until he was in his nineties. How inspirational! In my quest to continue my life path with God's grace I am looking for projects that I can do for the rest of my life. Life is one continuum and starting something new can possibly wake up dormant talents that can lead to a new career, interest or even a soul mate. This year is so much more than resolutions this year is about expansion, growth and insight to your true potential. So go out there and find your passion!

Your outings don't have to be expensive. It could be something like planting a vegetable garden in a little box by your kitchen window, or a small vegetable garden outside. You could go on the Internet and contact other fellow gardeners in your community. Find out where they meet, and go. Or you could visit some of the nurseries or botanical gardens in your city. Have one of the employees educate you about gardening.

Something artistic is always fun. Attending a play, or going to an art museum is always a fun adventure. One year I went to the Shakespearean Festival in Cedar City Utah. It was awesome! I saw the Lion in The Winter. My companion and I were so excited about the play. When we got back home we rented the movie.

Stepping out of your norm could be a little intimidating, but it could also be the very thing that will spark a new and powerful direction in your life. Don't just stop at thirty days. Add this into your life as your new reality.

MONTH 8

August: The Art of Doing Nothing

That's right! The art of doing nothing could be the most intimidating practice of all. The art of doing nothing can be life changing. The art of doing nothing gives you a big break from schedules and deadlines, etc. etc. The art of doing nothing teaches us to slow down and take life easy. The art of doing nothing refuels your engine and brings back humor and creativity.

When was the last time you just took some time out to daydream? I really don't mean for just a few minutes. But taking some real time out, time to listen to music, lie on the sofa, or sit in your back yard.

The world that we live in is in a constant state of activity! We hardly get anytime to breathe. When we are not working, we fill our lives up with stuff to do. If we are not absolutely busy, we often feel embarrassed or guilty that we have slowed down. This is not good news. Heart attacks are on the rise for women. Women are working long hours, and then coming home taking care of families. It is absolutely crazy!!!

I have a sister/friend, Batyah, who declares her Sabbath day. It starts from Friday evening to sundown Saturday evening. She goes shopping on Fridays. She makes sure she has paid her bills, cleaned her house, and all those necessary things that need to be done are done before sunset Friday. After the sun goes down she is done. From that time to Saturday evening she does not leave her house or engage in any physical activity. People can visit, she may read, or she might watch movies or even sleep.

Family members and friends are aware of her declaration. Of course if there is an emergency she will definitely be available. But she has said if it is not a life or death situation, she will not come out of her Sabbath. My friend said this simple practice has changed her life dramatically. She said it gives her time to refuel and to respect her life.

She has taken the time to honor her life, and people respect her time out. She has been practicing this for about 3 years. I can see the change; she really looks well rested and happy.

Now I know many of you will say I don't have time for this. I have work school, a husband, children, or care taker of aging parents,

We all have great responsibilities, but if we don't take the time to refuel and honor life, the outcome could lead to some unfavorable circumstances.

Now many of you might say I really can't take a full day of rest. But the point is to find the time. Many women have very active households. Many have demanding jobs and don't want to feel like they are neglecting husband or children.

Some of us have gone back to school and are also working full time. It's exhausting just thinking about all the demands on our time daily.

Here are some creative ways to schedule some down time:

1) Get your family involved. Sit down and talk to your husband and children, and plan some time for you. When your family understands the benefit of this time for yourself, it will help them see you in a different light. You are not just a mom and wife. You're a person with needs.

2) Create a lady cave. Men have caves, women can too. Get your family involved with creating a space just for you in the house. It could be anywhere from a small space to an entire room. You and your family can decorate your space with all of your favorite things. This could be a lot of fun.

3) Caution! Be real specific about your time, this is important. Everyone needs to know that this time and space is yours. Consistency is the key.

4) During this time get family members to agree to take care of each other and do some family chores. This leaves your mind free while you are having your down time.

5) This exercise is also crucial for single women as well, and especially for single mothers. Single women are busy and need time to recoup as well. If you are single and live alone, your home can be your woman cave.

6) Personal time away from your loved one, not as a care taker; but as an individual is vital. Several of my friends (included myself before my parents passing) are currently or have been care takers for aging parents. It is a noble and beautiful thing to do. But the care taker needs time out, so call upon trusting loving people who will support and help you take some time out.

7) Schedule some time away from the world. Let your friends and family know your time out schedule, so you can enjoy your space without interruption.

8) Single moms are earth angels (also single dads)! They have the responsibility of a two parent family. It's so necessary for single moms and dads to have their down time. Now your time will need planning. Get friends and family involved.

9) A lot of single moms have other single mom friends. You and your friends could help each other by scheduling specific times throughout the week. Then gather the kids and take turns on who watches them. This would allow each mom some down time, and could turn into a group effort.

10) Call on family members to pick up your kids for your time out, or if finances permit get a part-time nanny. Maybe even get a nanny for a day. (Now some people are not comfortable with people they do not know watching their children, even if a company is reputable. So do these activities according to your budget and comfort level).

11) This exercise is to create time for yourself, and not to create more stress. This is your choice so tailor it to your life. The caretaker can be in your house while you are relaxing. Or they can take the children for an outing for the day.

The art of doing nothing can be as creative and individual as you are. We all live different lives and have different circumstances in which we live. But this exercise will add rejuvenation to your life. It could also inspire creativity. In any case you have now added a new thing to your life, do this for thirty days. Now add this practice to your life as your new reality!

Review: You have added some new practices to your life! The art of first time experiences has brought back fun and a sense of adventure. It has made you smile and has ignited a new thing within you. Many of you have met new people, or started new interests. New pathways have opened up. The possibilities have no limits.

You have also added the art of doing nothing! Busy moms, wives, students, care takers and single parents all need a break. To actually set a time without interruption every week, is life changing indeed! A rested happy person is more productive and loving. The refueling of energy is a vital staple in the life of modern people. So congratulations you are living life intelligently and consciously. This is your year for your new reality.

MONTH 9

September - This month is the
art of pursuing dreams

Now that you have added time for relaxation, it's time to bring your dreams into reality. In the previous exercises doors open to pathways, and pathways open to dreams. Your space is decluttered. Your mind is free. You have scheduled time to do new things, and take some time out. Your creativity has been stimulated. Many of you have already embarked upon some new creative projects.

You have been doing exercises and practices that have been life changing. During these last months you've discovered a lot about your life. This could be the perfect time to do a possible career change, start a new business, or start a side business. During this process of reconnecting to your spirit you have expanded in your thinking and your way of being.

Many of you might tap into something artistic and creative. Maybe you have been inspired to reconnect to some things that you had let go of because of your responsibility to your family. Some of you might begin to write again. It could be a book that you always wanted to write. You might be inspired to do photography, to paint, or even cook again. I mean gourmet cooking. Not like the everyday cooking, but the kind of cooking when you use your special ingredients and invite your favorite friends over to enjoy a great evening. It could be an evening with a fun theme. A Moroccan theme is fun; you could style the room with huge colorful pillows, and use beautiful fabrics. Set a table in your living room, let the pillows be your seating, make finger foods, and put some exotic music on and dance. The possibilities are endless.

There are also cooking classes scheduled in different locations in every city. With all of the great cooking shows, cooking is very stylish and fun. Create evenings and gatherings periodically in your home. You could have your gourmet cooking at a friend's house and let them host. If it is in the summer time, dress up your back yard with music, candles, and colorful plates.

If the meal is in the winter, set up cozy spots in the house where people can talk and eat. Have dinner in front of your fire place with your loved one, or a few close friends.

Take the eating to a new level and visit the wine country. Go with friends, your spouse, or a buddy to different cities just for the purpose of finding great food.

Plan a dream trip, and plan it a year out. Call a travel agent, do your research. Read about the culture, the natives, the language, and the food. Find places that you want to explore and plan for it. While planning your trip always leave time on your vacation for doing something fun and spontaneous.

When I took my first trip to Europe, 4 years ago, it was my greatest adventure to date. This trip included three countries and four cities. It was one the most incredible trips of my life. My friends and I went to Venice and stayed in an 18th Century hotel. We saw our first Italian opera. In Paris we experienced the Notre Dame, the Louvre, and the Eiffel Tower. In Barcelona we saw our first flamenco dancer, he left us breathless! And finally in Rome we went to the Vatican, and saw the Sistine Chapel. What an incredible experience.

This trip took a lot of planning, and a lot brown paper bag lunches. I stopped getting manicures and pedicures. I did my own grooming, and this alone saved me some money. During that time I also avoided buying new clothes. I was very careful about spending. The trip was worth every sacrifice!

If you truly take a look at your spending, there are areas that you can eliminate for awhile in order to take your dream trip.

After eliminating some of these things, it's possible that you might find you can live without them. Freeing up this money can be the beginning of starting a dream savings account.

I purchased books about money and ways to stretch every dollar. I read a lot about finances, because in the past I haven't been a person that has been savvy with money. But the information was invaluable. I was determined to do some things that I had been dreaming of for a long time. It was time for change how I looked at money. Taking the time to do this research gave me some great information about money that I am still practicing today.

During the fall, traveling is typically cheaper. Arrange your time according to your time and budget.

This could be your year to buy that dream house, or change the décor in your home, or perhaps even do some remodeling.

This could be the time to go after the dream job. If so start preparing for it and make your move.

The thing you aspire to do doesn't have to be something huge. It depends on where you are in life. Possibly you might need to take quantum leaps and dramatically change your life. Perhaps you might need to take baby steps, or just do something that is very personal and special for yourself. Life could already be great, and by just adding this little thing could be the very component that brings you more joy. Even if you have had a tough year, and money is tight this is your time!

A special note: the world has been challenged economically. The projects and the suggestions that I make are just that, suggestions. This isn't about spending money this is about transformation. The world has challenged us all to live and think differently. This is about finding a new way to express your heart felt desires. So work on your dream, and do something daily that will bring you closer to it becoming a reality. When you have something to look forward to, it makes the pressures of life more bearable. The point is to bring the magic back into your life. It is really up to you. There are really no real instructions on how to manifest your dreams. Just do something that will bring you closer to bringing things into your reality. After 30 days it has become your new reality! Make dreaming and planning become a part of your lifestyle.

MONTH 10

The Power of Vision

Yes the power of vision! How can I talk about dreams, transformation, faith, and balance without mentioning vision. The word suggests something extraordinary.

When searching for the meaning of vision this is what the dictionary says:

1) The act or power of sensing with the eyes' sight

2) The act or power of anticipating that which will or may come to be; prophetic vision.

3) An experience in which a person, thing or event appears vividly or credibly to the mind, a thought not actually present, often under the influence of a divine or other agency; *a heavenly messenger appears in a vision.*

4) Unusual competence in discernment or perception; intelligent foresight.

Wow an unusual perception, not actually present but often under the influence of a divine agency the act of anticipating that which will come to be. Vision fuels dreams! Vision gives instruction and ideas on how to strategically plan and activate a dream.

No great thing has been produced without it. Greatness is born out of vision!

It sounds lofty, but just ask anyone who has ever accomplished their dream. They will tell you, with that glazed look and far away expression in their eyes, about a dream that first started in their heart and was later cultivated in their mind.

Everything in the material world started with vision. Things we see every day, the buildings, cars, houses, and even the whole technological world all started with a vision. The person creating the dream saw the vision in their mind and brought it to life.

In some cases you have heard people say they can feel or taste the dream. The first time I went to Paris, wasn't my first time. In my mind I had been to Paris a million times. I had seen and visited all of the famous landmarks in my head. In my mind I strolled down the Champs-Elysees and shopped on my way to a quaint bistro nearby. When I began to have sensory experiences, meaning the vision became almost palatable I had to go to Paris.

I could no longer just imagine Paris. I had to experience it in real time.

I have a young friend who is like a daughter to me. She was studying to become a forensic psychologist. She shared with me that she has a photographic memory. She said that she studies extremely hard, and when she takes her exams she can actually picture the words as they were written in her study materials. How incredible is that! What a great gift to have as a student. She sees the words in her mind. She has an incredible mind for detail, which will be essential in her work. Ms. Dutton has since moved forward, completed her degree, and now a psychologist.

The act of composing music really blows my mind too. How on earth does a composer compose a song? What the heck is that? The definition that mentioned divinity at work would truly describe this. Composers see music in their heads, and they transform what they see into notes. Those notes are transformed into melodies, played by instruments, and then we hear the music. It is truly incredible!

Scientists and inventors write complicated formulas, and create products that we use in everyday life. It has been said that Einstein saw the speed of light in a dream. Remember The Theory of Relativity, $E=mc2$? That formula manifested out of vision.

Pastors, leaders of countries, engineers, writers, architects, artist, athletes, and business people are visionaries too. In essence, I believe that vision is when the natural meets the divine. The conduit is the person that brings the vision into existence.

That thought makes me smile because everyone has vision. Everyone has dreams.

Note: Continue to integrate mind, body, and spirit practices; add dreams and visions, and watch how your life becomes more interesting and fulfilling.

MONTH 11

November: The art of gratitude; by words and acts

This is the month when the country celebrates being thankful. This is a time for family and friends. But truly make this a new Thanksgiving by trying something new and creating new traditions. Start your gratitude book, and keep this book with you everywhere you go. At random times, be in the moment and write down the gratefulness of what you are experiencing. Remember in the earlier chapter we discussed being in the present. This is a perfect time to jot down things that you see, and experience that move you. These treasures are what life is about! When you take time out to read what you are grateful for, it gives you a greater perspective about what is truly important. It also helps you to be sensitive and in tune to the gift of life.

Words have such impact on our lives. I think this is a great time to discuss word power.

The power of words -Proverbs 18:21: The tongue has the power of life and death and those who love it will eat its fruit.

Words have a powerful impact upon our world. They can be used to encourage and heal, or to create some unfavorable circumstances.

Just recently I watched two movies that were about words. The words that the characters spoke were prophetic. The characters in the story had bad results because of negative words which manifested in negative intent. The tongue has the power to bless or curse. (Genesis 1: 1-31) God spoke the world into existence. How powerful is that? The world manifested by God speaking it into existence. The scripture that has comforted me through divorce, single parenting, going back to college and getting a degree and so much more is the 23rd Psalm,

> *The Lord is my Sheppard I shall not want.*
> *He makes me lie down in green pasture;*
> *He leads me beside the still waters, He restores my soul.*
> *He leads me in the path of righteousness, for His name sake.*
> *Yea, though I walk through the valley of the shadow of death,*

I will fear no evil; for You are with me; Your rod and Your staff, they comfort me.
You prepare a table before me in the presence of my enemies.
You anoint my head with oil; My cup runs over.
Surely goodness and mercy shall follow me all the days of my life.
I will dwell in the house of the Lord forever.

The 23rd Psalm has kept me grounded over time and when I speak the words they have even more power. What are you creating by the words you speak? This is a great time of the year to think about that. Are you creating more in your life by speaking words of gratitude? Being grateful produces more abundance in life!

This season was specifically set for being thankful. But really the act of thankfulness goes far beyond a day. Remember this is the year for new things, a lifestyle change, so add the newness of expressing thankfulness in words and actions.

Remember, by physically engaging in giving you are creating the law of reciprocity. You want more love, give love. You want support give support. You want more money, give more money. You want more joy, give more joy. The major reason for giving is for the other person to benefit. But the giver benefits as well.

There are so many ways to express gratitude in new ways during this season. Make something tasty and leave it on your friend's door step. Write on beautiful paper why you are grateful for this person's friendship, and leave it with the tasty treats. We all respond to gratitude. Do this for multiple friends throughout the Thanksgiving season.

Give thank you cards to friends and people that have been supportive throughout the year. This could be a co-worker, people at a grocery store that you frequently shop at, the mechanic that fixes your car, or your baby sitter. Randomly send flowers to friends. The list is endless. By expressing gratitude, we open the doors to pathways of abundance.

Add acts of gratefulness to your new reality. Do this randomly throughout the year, not just during the Thanksgiving season. Do something for others, perfect strangers. It doesn't have to be something huge, but it could be, it just depends. Every gesture of gratitude is great. The idea is to be effective in the lives of people.

Be a blessing!

This is a great time also for reflection. You've progressed in amazing ways. Get quiet and wrap yourself up in a wonderful comforter. And light your fireplace. If you don't have a fireplace, get some inexpensive scented candles and light them. (Do this at sunrise or sunset). Put on some of your favorite music. Busy moms, do this during your down time in your mom cave. And for wives, do this when hubby is working, sleeping, or engaged in some other activity. I might also add that you get your favorite drink, water, hot chocolate, eggnog, or coffee. Also celebrate with your favorite foods. This is your own personal time to celebrate!

Now reflect upon what you have learned so far. Many of you have really stepped way out of the box, and it has blown your own mind.

A lot of healing has taken place. You really didn't know how depleted you really were. Some of you knew, but you just couldn't get a handle on it. You have blossomed in ways that you didn't even know were possible.

The funny thing about change is everyone close to you has changed too. The way they interact with you has totally changed. You taught them through your actions who you are!

 I am pretty sure you have inspired people around you to investigate and create a new path and a new reality for themselves.

Finding new pathways for living has taken a lot of imagination, but also a lot of courage. Changing is a lot more challenging than just talking about it. You actually decided to do something about it. That alone is an extraordinary feat.

Explore how your personal chapters have truly changed! Explore how you were able to use chapters one, two, and three in reflection. These chapters made it possible for you to let go of the unnecessary in your life. Also celebrate how you were able to change your chapter four into a dynamic course!

What you have created for yourself is a fuller and richer life. On the back of my business card it reads "A More Powerful You!" The change did not make you into another person the change reconnected you back to your core back to your real and true spirit. You feel more comfortable in your skin. The change is you, but a more vibrant you.

Throughout the Thanksgiving Holiday, while you and your family gather together take some time to reflect upon this dynamic year in your life. The year you decided to embark upon an authentic path. The year you reconnected to your spirit and found your new reality.

Review: In the previous chapters you focused on the art of stepping out on your dream and the art of gratitude.

Bringing dreams into reality does require some work and planning. But it also requires a willingness to make the daydream into the real thing. You have taken leaps and bounds this year to find your authentic self, and create new pathways while reconnecting to your core spirit. Wow! Now you have added to your new reality. You Added those dreams that have been dormant for years.

Manifesting your dreams adds new excitement to life. It gives you something to look forward to. Life can be tough at times. It can be a challenge to live life, and continue to keep dreams alive. The dream has been placed in your heart and mind for a reason.

This entire new journey has been about finding a way to be the real you. You now have a lot to be grateful for. The art of being grateful is just the icing on the cake!

Look for opportunities to express gratitude and to be grateful. Keep your pad and pencil near you so you can jot down these precious moments as you continue to experience your new reality.

MONTH 12

December: In the beginning

You are almost back at the starting point again. What an incredible year! Whew! Did you ever think that your life could change so dramatically? Joy has a new interpretation. In Western culture, having a lot of money and possessions is considered rich. I am not saying that having money and wealth are to be frowned upon. We need money and to work hard and achieve is a noble thing. But what I am saying is that looking deep within, and finding a way to enrich your own life as well as the people around you, is a great investment.

This is the designated season for giving. This is Jesus Christ's birthday, and the ritual is to give and receive presents. Truly every season is the season of giving. But because of the investment that you have made in your life during this year, you are able to give more and be more.

You have reconnected to your core, and you have expanded and grown in leaps and bounds. To be a better you is a great gift to the world. There is no price on that!

This season, you and your family get to experience a richer you! They benefit from the work that you engaged in on your journey to *Finding Your Authentic Path*.

Let's do a recap of everything that you have learned during this incredible year. All of these steps are taking you to your anniversary date. This New Year's Eve will be extraordinary because of the work that you did this year! You will have a lot more to celebrate, and the coming year will be more than just empty resolutions. You have made real and concrete changes in your life. These significant changes are your new normal. Now let's look back.

In the first chapter you started with taking inventory and making an assessment of your life. This exercise was for the purpose of making real life adjustments in areas of your life that were not authentic. You started by looking at your life as four chapters. With the past being the first chapter of your life. You begin editing your fourth chapter by using your first chapter as a teacher. Your second and third chapters were used as a way to salvage what was good and to let go of what was obsolete in your present life. You challenged old behaviors, attitudes, and thinking. You took a look at yourself in relationships. This was a courageous step forward. You were done with empty promises you had made to yourself. You wanted to experience real change and you did it!

In the next chapter you took a deeper look at letting go and surrendering to God. This action was also a bold step. While you were surrendering, you took practical steps to change behaviors that created pain in your life. You did the work to make the adjustments, and added new skills to your arsenal. Excellent!

You continued to build by recognizing the power of balance. You learned and gained understanding of the pathology of what extreme living can produce. The example given was that of a juggler having too many balls in the air, and how those balls came crashing down when life became out of balance. Balance gives life a chance to integrate and apply what you've learned while using your time wisely. Balance enriches life.

Purpose was added to the skill building. The acknowledgment of purpose being the blue print that God created for you to follow. The tailoring of life decisions, led to activating your purpose.

We examined what was needed to continue your path. Faith and perseverance were discussed as the fuel to keep you motivated. We discussed how faith will keep you through the times when there is no physical evidence of what you believe in. That in itself is a powerful concept. Faith is mysterious, but it is real. When faith is ignited the impossible becomes possible.

In chapter three, we studied the art of letting go and living in the present. Present living causes you to maximize the human experience. We looked at the benefits of living in the present. When we live in the present, we can experience the benefits of lowering the stress level and being focused upon the now. We learned that when we are living in the present, we are able to experience and appreciate more. When we are living in the present our minds are not being divided and we are able to give our full attention to what is happening around us. Our awareness level is heightened. The body is more relaxed which is a great benefit to our oxygen flow, and blood pressure. We can experience more joy because we are paying attention. We discussed how living in the now is an aspect of letting go. Which means letting go of future and past thoughts while you are absorbing what you are experiencing in the present.

In chapter four the art of meditation and prayer was introduce. Meditation is a deeper level of being and concentration. We talked about meditation as the art of being in silence. The silence created the space for the mind to rest and to receive instructions from God. When the mind rests, it provides room for clarity and revelation. It was even suggested that meditation could cause more productivity and the mind to become more efficient. Because of the manic busyness in our society, meditation is a form of listening, while prayer is a form of talking to

God. God is always speaking to us. Through quiet focused time, we are able to talk to God. Through prayer and listening we find the best solutions to our issues. The word of God, the bible, is his blue print for living. All three practices combined solidify the powerful process of transformation.

In chapter five we talked about the power of forgiveness and its benefits. Forgiveness pardons a person of the wrong act they committed against someone. Forgiveness is letting go. Forgiveness is grace. Grace heals the wound of the person causing the pain, and the person who received the pain.

Forgiveness allows the injured person to move forward, and releases the other person of their wrongdoing. Not forgiving holds people in captivity. We also talked about the physical benefits of forgiveness, and how the body responds with ease. However when there is unforgiveness, the body responds with disease. We discussed how forgiveness unties God's hand, and how he creates space for a better future for the person who forgives. Last but not least, we discussed the importance of forgiving yourself. It requires the same principal of letting go of past errors, and utilizing the past as a teacher. Holding on to the past prevents you from moving on and enjoying the present by making better choices for the future.

In chapter six, after making space in your heart and mind through forgiveness, we moved on to taking actions to create physical space in your living area. We began by taking inventory. Just like you took inventory and assessment of your life in chapter one, you duplicated the same in your living area.

By letting go of items you no longer needed, you were able to create new space. You were able to discard old items, and you were able to give away items to people who could benefit.

Chapter seven was the fun chapter: You let go of the past, created new space, and you moved on to creating something new in your life. The art of something new brought back magic and a sense of adventure.

We discussed the possibility of going back to school, remodeling your house, taking new classes, gourmet cooking, planting a garden, painting, writing, and starting a new business or a new hobby. The art of something new held no rules. The simple act of adding some fun to your life was the goal.

Chapter eight is one of my favorite chapters, the art of doing nothing! Spending time relaxing and daydreaming was the only requirement. This practice is intimidating to busy people. But slowing down and relaxing is the point. We discussed creating spaces in your home designed for your down time. We also talked about getting your family involved in this process so they can be a part of respecting your time out.

In chapter nine, the art of pursuing your dreams assisted you with also bringing magic back into your life. We looked at how so many people do the responsible thing in their lives, by taking care of themselves and their families. By taking some time to pursue something that has been close to your heart, creates another dimension. Pursuing dreams takes the pressure off of everyday living and add balance to life.

Chapter 10 speaks about vision. How can you manifest dreams without vision? We talked about how everything seen in the natural world started with vision. It is created in the mind first, then acted upon.

Chapter 11 is the chapter on gratitude. Thanksgiving is the designated season for thankfulness in America, but the discussion was to go beyond just a day. We talked about keeping a little notebook close to you, so you could record throughout your days what you are grateful for. We talked about the power of giving, and the principle of reciprocity. The spiritual and practical aspects of giving are powerful. Giving benefits both the giver and the receiver.

It is more blessed to give than to receive.

Chapter 12 is the beginning. You are at the finish line, but you are starting a whole new life! You have begun a new life, and this year you are able to give the gift of a more vibrant you. You no longer have to make empty declarations and resolutions. Because you have done the work already, this process of *Finding Your Authentic Path* has opened new doors and new pathways for your life.

When you look back over this year and the process you have just gone through, you will be able to see how all the chapters are really intertwined. How the spiritual and practical work together that brought about wholeness. When the mind, body, and spirit are working together in harmony, it creates wellness on so many levels.

The assessment in chapter one was a type of cleansing, allowing you to start off the new year with a clean slate. Faith was the fuel, purpose was the blueprint, and balance was the flavor. Letting go released you from the past so you could enjoy the present, and make good decisions for the future. Meditation and prayer gave you clarity and forgiveness gave you peace while renewing your path. Discarding old things was the reflection in the practical of what you had already done in the spiritual. The art of doing nothing opened up pathways to dreams. Pursuing dreams brought them into the practical, and vision gave you the ability to see. Gratefulness is the result of the hard work, and wholeness is the result of you moving in a full circle. The end has become the new beginning for you.

365 Days to Authenticity is a powerful journey to getting you back to your original intent. My prayer for you is that this journey continues for the rest of your life, and you will continue to create and manifest great things.

Printed in the United States
By Bookmasters